# DISCOVER
# Forests

### by Barbara Brannon

## Table of Contents

# Introduction

**Trees** are in **forests**. **Plants** are in forests. **Animals** are in forests.

# Words to Know

animals

forest fires

forests

people

plants

trees

See the Glossary on page 22.

3

# Where Are Forests?

Forests are in Australia.

N
W E
S

Australia

▲ This forest is in Australia.

Forests are in Europe.

▲ This forest is in Europe.

Forests are in Asia.

Europe

Asia

N
W    E
S

▲ This forest is in Asia.

## Chapter 1

Forests are in Africa.

▲ This forest is in Africa.

It's A Fact

Forests are important to people. People get food from forests. People get wood from forests.

nuts    bananas    coconuts    wood

Forests are in North America.

▲ This forest is in North America.

Forests are in South America.

North
America

South
America

▲ This forest is in South America. 7

# What Is In Forests?

Koalas are in forests.

▲ Koalas live in forests.

Tigers are in forests.

▲ Tigers live in forests.

Bears are in forests.

▲ Bears live in forests.

Elephants are in forests.

▲ Elephants live in forests.

Birds are in forests.

▲ Birds live in forests.

## Then and Now

Many elephants lived in African forests. African forest elephants are dying. Not many elephants are in African forests now.

Snakes are in forests.

▲ Snakes live in forests.

## Did You Know?

Anacondas live in rivers. Anacondas climb trees, too. Anacondas live in South American forests.

# What Do Forest Fires Hurt?

**Forest fires** hurt trees.

Forest fires hurt plants.

Forest fires hurt animals.

▲ **Forests burn.**

Forest fires hurt homes.

▲ **Forests burn.**

Forest fires hurt **people**.

▲ Forests burn.

## Did You Know?

Lightning causes some forest fires.

# Conclusion

Forest fires hurt Earth.

# Concept Map

## Forests

### Where Are Forests?

| |
|---|
| Australia |
| Europe |
| Asia |
| Africa |
| North America |
| South America |

### What Is In Forests?

| |
|---|
| koalas |
| tigers |
| bears |
| elephants |
| birds |
| snakes |

# What Do Forest Fires Hurt?

trees

plants

animals

homes

people

21

# Glossary

**animals** living things that can move around

*Forest fires hurt **animals**.*

**forest fires** burning of wooded areas

*Forest fires hurt plants.*

**forests** areas of trees, plants, and animals

*Trees are in **forests**.*

**people** human beings

*Forest fires hurt **people**.*

**plants** living things that can not move around

*Forest fires hurt **plants**.*

**trees** plants with trunks

*Forest fires hurt **trees**.*

# Index